Planning and Development; Changing the way we travel

Cruise liner seen in the port of Cannes

By Paul Spelzini

A look at the world of planning and development, how travel has changed over the years and how the way we travel is likely to change in the coming years and decades.

Written and edited by Paul Spelzini

This publication may contain some adult material not suitable for reading by very young children. The book may contain some technical terms, and other phraseology which may not be in current use, as it deals with some developing technologies across the globe.

This books depicts certain events and facts, but any similarity to other real events, past current or future is purely co-incidental.

Contents;

1. The Situation before the Oil Crisis in 1974

Prior to 1974, travel was generally well ordered and followed the social classes worldwide. There were relatively few cars on the road at that time, although car usage was starting to grow appreciably in the developed countries.

People generally walked where possible to both keep fit and active, and many used public transport which was in good supply and reliable and relatively cheap at that time, compared to today in real terms.

There were well established bus networks nationally, and internationally in the developed countries, although many third world countries were still relatively undeveloped at this stage.

New towns had sprung up in the UK and other nations mainly during the post WW2 period up to the mid-1960s. This fuelled the demand for travel.

About this time the demand for foreign holidays started to grow, but it was not until the advent of Laker Airways and Freddie Laker, that kick started the low cost air revolution that we know today.

The United States at this time had a good network of express coach services, as air services had not become fully established at this time. Rail in America was still well used, but losing ground due to long travel times, giving way to the car ultimately.

Freight also had right of way on rail in the US and Canada which was a problem as this tended to block the development of high speed rail which occurred later on in Europe during the 1980s.

In the UK there was a good network of green line express coaches in London and the South east counties, and a network of buses countrywide, which were generally well used.

Of course architecture was starting to develop into modern forms at this time, with high rise living becoming the norm in many cities, with point blocks and large social housing estates to replace slums and back to back housing which was condemned.

However the traditional street pattern disappeared, and with it travel needs changed as people had to walk between blocks on high level walkways in places like London's South Bank. These were described as a concrete jungle, although the architectural community regarded these as award winning triumphs for the professions.

The need for faster living and travelling further afield led to the development of new strategies for travel around this time. British Rail as it was then developed the 4 strand strategy for future rail travel following the Beeching cutbacks of the 1960s in the UK, to give the rail Industry a clearer and more secure future.

An older 737 seen with Britannia, a mainstay of the airline from the 1970s until taken over by Monarch.

At this time there was little incentive to be fuel efficient, so vehicles were petrol and oil or diesel fired, and not particularly clean in terms of emissions.

Likewise shipping was still using oil at this time, with many older ships still in use since the war, so these were ageing visibly.

In Europe the rail networks were still using steam power until the late 1960s, when it started to decline gradually across the continent. However steam was still in use in Asia and the America's until much later. Diesel traction became the norm in many industrialised countries, but electrified rail lines started to appear on the busiest routes, due to the cleaner and more efficient use of power.

Settlements traditionally had been very close knit in the past, but the trend towards modern new towns, which were more spread out required a different type of transport network for this situation.

Older style buses could not cope so well with diverse and modern housing over a wide area. This led to the growth of the private car, which started to grow in popularity as cities spread outwards into suburbs, which the traditional bus and train services were not adept at serving.

The traditional rail networks had not changed much since before the Second World War in the industrialised countries, with set service patterns which had become established over many years.

The same comment applied to bus services particularly around London which had become very established over many years.

However rising costs and development pressures in the late 1960s led to the introduction of one man buses and the ubiquitous Leyland National, which became the mainstay of London Country and many regional bus services for many years, taking over form older models which had held sway in many cases since the 1950s.

The ubiquitous Leyland National seen at St. Albans Abbey station

The bus networks were very good generally with good coverage and frequent services, even on many rural routes at this time.

Cycling was in its infancy as a sport, with very little specific provision for cyclist on public roads, except perhaps in the new towns outside London where cycle routes and grade separated junctions had been created and been popular.

Walking continued to be popular with many public rights of way and footpaths and bridleways still in existence today, which had been in existence for many years. Walking abroad was less common as foreign travel was in its infancy in those days.

Rail services continued to be popular, although rail was in decline up to the late 1960s and early 1970s. This led to a spate of station closures, and campaigns to save railways which would otherwise disappear.

Unfortunately a number did disappear, and ironically there are no calls to reopen lines closed by Beeching to due increased demand. Railways had to reinvent themselves to become more economic and efficient, as efficiency had declined to an all-time low.

Airlines were in their infancy but taking some of the railways' passengers, along with cars, and trucks were taking freight off of the railways and onto the roads.

To counteract decline, the British railways board had to act and fast to stop decline and give the rail Industry a future.

New developments in architecture led to development of the container for freight, using metal palletised containers approximately 12 feet long. These could be interchangeable between road and rail, and became an instant success.

They could also be carried by sea, and this revolutionised the way freight was carried from the late1960's onwards. This also had some unplanned effects in that traditional rail and road ferries started to disappear as containers became the mode of choice for many freight companies.

First freight train from China to UK
Yiwu to London
January 2017

Barking-China intermodal train reinventing the ancient 'silk road'

Meanwhile on rail, British rail came up with a 4 point plan to develop train travel into the next century, and make it more efficient and modern.

Most trains at this time were still locomotive hauled worldwide with carriages, rather than multiple units which are now commonplace except for freight.

The 4 main concepts for rail included;

-A small multiple unit for local train services known as a Pacer;

-A diesel-electric heavy goods locomotive for freight;

-A high speed multiple unit train with diesel electric engines powered at each end

- and an electric multiple unit for London area third rail and overhead line services.

Some of these concepts were very successful, and indeed some of the original high speed trains are still in service today, albeit with new more efficient engines.

However the Pacer local train services were underdeveloped and remained in service too long, and showed their age.

It was also in the early 1970s that the Trans Europe Express or TEE concept as it was known was developed linking major European cities by a high speed train service for the first time.

The Orient Express and named trains of the past had developed a good reputation but the age of opulence was giving way to speed, in competition with the developing airlines in Europe and America at that time.

Many of these TEE trains were conventional locomotive hauled carriages running at high speed on dedicated routes.

However the Swiss developed a truly revolutionary type of train, being the first quadri-voltage unit in service anywhere.

This operated between France, Switzerland Germany and Italy using 1500 volts DC, 2500 volts DC, 15000 volts AC and 25000 volts AC.

This used 4 pantographs or current collecting devices, with a permanently coupled 6 car unit with corridors-a first in many terms.

Swiss TEE quadri-voltage set seen at Chur, Switzerland in the 1970s

Shipping at this time was still very traditional with ships split according to function. So there were a plethora of coasters, freighters, ferries, passenger ships, liners, river cruisers, plus military ships, etc.

Many ships dated from the war, so were old and fuel inefficient. However the growing demand for container traffic forced a rethink, and a new generation of containers hips started to be built to replace ageing ferries and conventional cargo ships, which had had their day.

This resulted in a boom in container traffic and ports like Tilbury and Felixstowe, but marked a sharp decline in traditional tidal docklands like the port of London which went into almost terminal decline.

This obviously had a considerable effect upon the local jobs market, with a shift towards the new transport arrangement and away from declining industries.

The shift on rail to diesel and electric traction also saw a shift in the use of coal, which went into decline and resulted in a shift away from traditional fossil fuels, due to increasing prices, and competition from developing countries which were cheaper.

The pace of change gathered momentum and eventually led to the Oil Crisis in 1974, where the price of Oil soared, and caused a knee jerk reaction in industrialised countries, which up to that point had been heavily reliant on coal and Oil.

2.1974–1986 and Deregulation of the Markets

The Oil Crisis in 1974 sparked a world-wide economic crisis, the likes of which had not been seen before.

Developing and Industrialised countries which had enjoyed unlimited growth based on cheap oil supplies since the end of the second world war, suddenly found themselves held to ransom effectively as the hostage to high prices.

Combined with political upheavals and changing social conditions, this caused a 3 day working week in the UK, and rapid reassessment of travel needs and oil supplies.

Many loss making industries and rural travel networks were cut back appreciably, and rail services curtailed. Queues of vehicles developed at petrol stations across the UK, but also in Europe and elsewhere.

Politically the world was going through the Cold War, although America had its own oil supplies so was less affected than the UK and Europe by the Oil Crisis in relative terms.

This crisis only hastened the shift away from public transport towards the private car and the internal combustion engine.

However the fuel crisis did trigger an interest in alternative fuel technologies, and sparked the beginning of the alternative and ambient energy industries, which have now grown to considerable size world-wide as a result.

Cuts in transport costs, meant that bus conductors became an endangered species, and interest in cycling, motorcycling, scooters and other forms of transport took off. One man buses became the norm very quickly in both cities and rural areas.

With oil and diesel becoming relatively more expensive, plans to electrify busy rail lines were accelerated out of necessity.

During this period the East Coast mainline in England was electrified during the late 1970s, and extended eventually to Scotland.

Many of the remaining rail routes in the South east were electrified, with relatively few now operated by diesel. However routes outside London are still mainly diesel operated even today.

In the developing world the use of coal still prevailed and labour was cheap, so practices remained pretty much the same, as they were not so affected by the Oil crisis as the Industrialised nations.

However pollution levels in the developing world were becoming a concern regarding climate change and pollution generally.

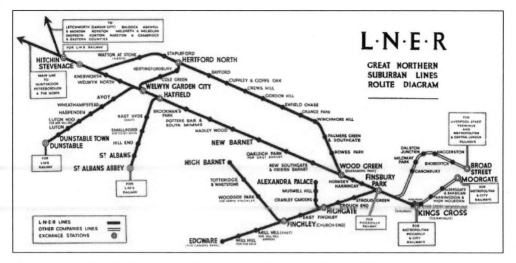

London and North Eastern railway suburban map from 1950.

Many of these routes closed by the mid to late1970s leaving just the main line and Hertford branch remaining today.

As the world of travel grew after the recession of the mid 1970's caused by the Oil Crisis, new types of travel started to gain ground.

One of these was the high speed train which became a commercial success, and brought rail into competition with short haul flights, where it had an advantage in not having lengthy check in and sometimes lengthy baggage pick up times at out of town airports.

It was in France that the High Speed train really came to the fore, opening up the Cote d'Azur from Paris via Lyon, which previously had been a slow, and all day journey.

This later developed into Eurostar which was operating in the UK by 1994, but had been operating in France since 1984, a decade earlier.

The British high speed diesel train went on to become a commercial success story, speeding up UK rail travel and reducing short haul air travel demand in the UK and near European coasts eventually.

The Optare minibus which became very popular after deregulation.

Other changes were happening worldwide with the deregulation of the financial and bus markets in the UK, which had become very static for many years and were in need of modernisation.

The introduction of computers allowed the revolution in financial services and travel to take place, initially in the UK but it soon spread to America and Europe and the far-east markets too.

In the UK, the change from a regulated bus market to a deregulated market saw competition emerge outside London for the first time in many years.

There was a minibus revolution with expensive large buses giving way to smaller, more flexible minibuses.

New networks of these sprang up, even in London where some traditional routes were replaced by Optare minibuses on new 'Hoppa' routes.

These were centred on suburban town centres such as Orpington, Barnet, Harrow, Walthamstow, Greenford, Kingston, etc.

Outside London, a notable weekday network of 6no. half hourly minibus routes sprang up in Welwyn Hatfield, which traditionally had fairly poor bus coverage, and proved very popular until it was taken over by Arriva in the late 1990s and reverted back to conventional buses.

That was a shame as a great social experiment and success was lost to recent history, with relatively little trace of it remaining.

A bus displaying a Herts County council contract board after deregulation

Deregulation had its critics, as it generated competition, which drove down fares and drove up frequencies on busy routes. However, it left some areas with no commercial bus coverage at all. So it was left to councils to decide to tender services they considered 'socially necessary'.

The definition of socially necessary has changed though. Councils regarded it as hospitals and rural areas. Bus operators tend to regard it now as retail and schools being 'socially necessary' which is very different.

In the Lea Valley for instance, commercial services abounded along the A1000 Hertford Road, with competition between London Country, the incumbent operator; London Buses, and small independents. However Hertford Heath, a small town between Hoddesdon and Hertford was a reduced to an hourly contract service.

Deregulation also saw London Buses, a nationalised company at it was then, go into competition with other nationalised companies in the form of London Country subsidiaries outside London.

This resulted in some fascinating new short lived ventures, such as the 310A from Enfield to Hertford; the 406 from Kingston to Epsom. The 290 and 216 were registered as commercial, but London Buses' 218 from Kingston –Staines via Epsom became London Country's 427 instead and was deregistered.

The preparation for deregulation also gave bus operators and financial services new markets to move into, and an opportunity to ditch loss making sectors and services, often picked up by councils and others at a later date.

Old steam railways are now making a comeback as tourist attractions

Travel by air and other modes though remained fairly static, with little development in air travel until later, with the advent of the low cost carriers.

Rail travel continued to develop, and saw the wider introduction of electric services, which we regaining ground across Europe and even in the UK.

The only place electrification failed notably was in the United States where some previously electrified east coast routes went back to diesel on the basis of cost, but this was seen by environmentalists as a backward, if temporary, step.

Happily high speed Amtrak services have been subsequently introduced between Boston, New York, Washington and Philadelphia.

However much of the United States remains surprisingly backward in terms of its infrastructure investment, with much of it still dating from the 1950s and 1960s, and is now showing its age.

This will cost billions of dollars to modernise, as most of the US rail network is still powered by fossil fuels notably diesel and oil, not sustainable fuels.

United States infrastructure can be seen in contrast to places like Vancouver, Canada that now boast a modern cable stayed metro bridge just outside the city.

Compare this to many rusting steel girder bridges dating from World War 2 which still carry rail and road routes across large swathes of the United States.

Conversely infrastructure in the developing world rates from basic in places like India to state of the art in parts of China and Japan.

However there are huge variations across the world and even within some countries in standards of infrastructure and levels of services provided.

The one thing that deregulation has shown, is that by computerising the marketplace, it actually expands the overall market and makes it more efficient.

This tends to generate more jobs, although the nature of those jobs has changed from production to managing and regulating in terms of role.

This has created some degree of repetition and deskilling which is unfortunate. However it is the growth of the service sector including buses, which has grown significantly.

However excess competition, has led to a decline in demand for UK bus use since deregulation; except in London where still regulated, but using a route or block tendering system instead.

Much of the ageing transport infrastructure in North America particularly will need replacement - a truly massive project

3. 1986-2000 and the Millennium

With deregulation came a surge in market demand and service provision world-wide, although this was not always seen as being healthy necessarily.

One side effect of bus deregulation was an increase in traffic levels. The traffic commissioner in the UK had powers to regulate areas where congestion was a problem, but this led to a marked growth in traffic levels on UK roads.

Deregulation also led to a boom in freight traffic and consequent road freight traffic levels too.

Gradually the size and weight of Heavy Good Vehicles using roads, certainly in the UK, across Europe and the United States grew from medium to supersized; and axle loads were increased from 25 to 44 tonnes, which traditional roads found hard to handle, resulting in increased wear and tear and costs of repair.

Likewise rail freight loadings increased too, with double decker trains appearing in Europe and the United States, which have a larger loading gauge than the United Kingdom.

The Channel Tunnel opened in 1994 and with it trade with Europe and the EU soared.

It was now possible to send rail freight direct to and from Europe and beyond without shipping or using air for the first time.This revolutionised the way products were delivered and processed.

The expansion of high speed rail required new types of rail routes designed for higher line speeds. This required wider clearances, TBM signalling systems in cab, and straighter routes than traditional rail routes.

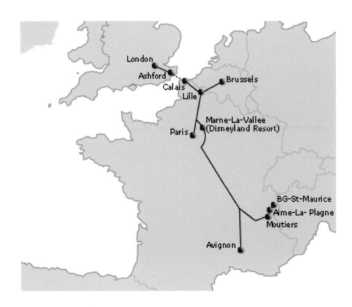

The Eurostar network expanded to the South of France

Many established rail routes were based on Victorian principles, and often were taken around a landowners' estate, resulting in either a tunnel or a sharp bend to avoid a particular estate, who may have objected to the railway originally.

Obviously in the modern world this can no longer be allowed to occur, otherwise rail and road routes could be held to ransom by unreasonable land owners or objectors deliberately causing delays, as has happened with airport growth.

The period immediately after deregulation saw a period of consolidation, with bedding down of new deregulated financial services and bus services alike.

This period also saw the introduction of the idea of franchising rail services which became prevalent after the Millennium.

There was also the break up and sell off of London Buses, and the National Bus Company outside London.

This involved the sell-off of valuable bus garage sites for housing development in urban areas, although this has since proved to be a mistake in retrospect.

In places like St. Albans of Finchley, the loss of strategically important garage sites has led to calls for these to be replaced by new Municipal undertakings, under the new Buses Act if permitted, or franchising to plug gaps which have not been satisfactorily filled.

The growth in road Traffic was relentless with road space becoming at a premium towards the Millennium. This saw a rise in traffic restrictions and parking restrictions and parking charges generally.

On the rails, the Eurostar network was born in 1994 with the completion of the Channel Tunnel, which had taken 5 years to build and opened with the first cross channel train service.

Freight services soon followed and we now have a Barking to Zhengzhou service which could be running up to once a week in future, as well as car transporters between Italy, Germany and the UK.

It was hoped that a Euro-night service would follow Eurostar, but this hit technical problems, such as services to the Great Western would need to be diesel hauled which would be slow.

Also the demand for Euro-night services did not match the daytime services, and overnight travel patterns were very different, so the idea was eventually dropped.

However what was a success was an experimental service to the new Disneyland Paris resort, which started as an occasional service but has now become a regular destination.

Demand for cheap skiing holidays boomed, and the idea of running an overnight service to Bourg St, Maurice and Moutiers in the Alps proved a popular one over the winter months, enabling young people to travel on a budget for a low cost skiing holiday in the Les Arcs range.

The new South Eastern High Speed Hitachi train at St. Pancras on 22nd July 2009-the first day of test operation to Ebbsfleet with the author

Fitness campaigns started to abound, as the new found growth in computers caused youngsters and others to become more sedentary in playing computer games.

Campaigns to encourage walking and mini-marathons to encourage fitness became popular. Gym membership saw a rise, but road traffic still saw the highest growth figures.

Buses on the other hand were facing a slow decline after deregulation, with competition for traffic increasing. Operators went back to larger vehicles operating less frequently due to rising costs.

Competition continued sometimes in unlikely places in the UK, and the traffic commissioner had to step in to regulate congestion in places like Oxford and Glasgow.

Another trend was to use older vehicles to save money, so the average age of vehicles started to increase on the roads, leading to higher emissions and pollution for a while, until more modern engine standards were adopted.

The UK was lagging behind much of Europe where high speed rail had been established since the 1980s. A map shows how extensive the system already was when Eurostar started its operations in the mid-1990s.

High speed rail map of Europe showing UK and Eastern Europe lagging

4. The Millennium to the Present day

After the Millennium, travel became more varied with arise in cycling, which achieved wider audience through Olympic successes.

Walking was established, but became more accessible as rights of way opened up giving new vistas and walks.

Road traffic continued its relentless rise, with our cities becoming more and more clogged up day by day, even at weekends which previously had been fairly quiet.

A number of initiatives were tried after the Millennium to boost non-car transport. These included the launch of new bus tickets at weekends, low cost rail tickets and deals available off peak.

There were even some excursion tickets available combining cheap train travel with visits to stately homes, excursions, special events and restaurants, which became very popular.

So much so, that this was the making of the 'last minute.com' brand, and a number of organisations specialising in this area, such as rail excursion travel and red letter days, virgin etc.

This also spread internationally to become big business with the likes of award winning Great Rail Journeys (formerly British Rail International of course). This business has spread significantly to take in many countries and rail excursions now.

In 2007, the rail excursion business and volunteer restored rail lines were so successful, that regular steam excursions returned to the main line.

This also saw the commissioning of the first new modern steam locomotive called 'Tornado' built at a cost of £3M, since Evening Star was rolled out in the early 1950s, and was assumed to be the last of its kind.

The slow decline of the UK bus industry was matched by a switch to rail, and a steady increase in ridership by rail. This was growing year on year such that some lines were struggling to cope with demand.

In London, the Silver link franchise came up for renewal also in 2007. However the Mayor of London bid to take over all rail lines in London eventually, with a big expansion of London Overground as it became known.

This resulted in the construction of a new line through east London, to south London, and new corridor trains for both the tube subsurface lines and London Overground.

This has proved very successful, and soon led to the lengthening of these trains to 5 coaches to cope with soaring demand.

New class 378 dual voltage London Overground train seen at West Brompton

In the world of bus travel, things were not so good with a number of services being deregistered and taken over as contracts, resulting in some withdrawals of lesser used routes.

This process was slow at first, but accelerated after the financial crash of 2008, with a need for local authorities to save money on budgets.

This resulted in a round of cuts initially in 2011, but this has grown in 2015 to the present day where 30% of services in some areas have gone.

A number of new initiatives have been tried to try and reverse the decline. This included hybrid and electric buses, which have proved expensive and not always reliable in use.

New types of service have emerged such as community buses and coach travel. Private school travel has grown, but private school bus provision and retail bus services have tended to have the most success.

Whilst services outside London have slowly declined, services inside London have grown steadily with consistent usage. This had led to further investment and newer vehicles than outside the capital.

In Europe and elsewhere, new initiatives were being introduced since 2008 such as the Microbus. This electric 10 seat Minibus has proved very popular in France, Italy and to a lesser extent in Germany.

This has reversed the decline in those countries, and a joined up system in Switzerland between rail, bus and cable car means that connectivity is assured whatever mode is used.

Gruau 10 seat electric free Microbus seen in Biarritz 2014, funded by tourism

The model used for financing services in Europe differs from the UK. This uses conventional commercial single deck buses, occasional longer distance coach routes, but Microbuses for tourist services, sponsored by the regional tourist budget.

Some Microbus services are operated free of charge to tourists or residents with a residents' card as an incentive to use the bus, rather than the car. Perhaps that is something we need to adopt more widely.

In Portland USA, public transport is fairly advanced with a mix of electric and hybrid buses, bendy buses for longer distance trips as well as modern trams.

There are still some issues such as the cable car does not operate evenings or Sundays; but links the hospital and river front town centre areas direct, whereas a car journey is up a steep hill.

Stored value cards are widely used and popular, and smartcards will eventually replace cash on all UK buses by 2022 it is hoped, using the EVM agreement (Electronic Visa and Master card).

More novel forms of transport have sprung up such as the rickshaw taxi in London, and electric bikes for the elderly. People also use skateboards, in line skates, etc.

but these are not mainstream forms of transport, and are still exposed to the weather.

That may explain why Vespa scooters are a big hit with young people in Italy, but less so in London and northern European countries.

Urban cable car in Portland, USA used to reduce road traffic

With greater use of contactless cards in London now on the tube, DLR, London Overground and bus; it is only a matter of time that cash may disappear from public transport altogether.

This would make public transport more attractive if people don't have to search for change. Oyster and other smartcards have already proved popular in London and other cities also.

If this could be rolled out to all transport, then it would make using the car seem less attractive, particularly as congestion gets worse in busy areas.

With buses, more investment is needed as private bus networks such as schools are booming but public buses are in slow decline. Without investment they will gradually disappear from some areas, like they already have done.

Some communities have rallied around to operate and fund their own services. Which has been a success in places. The 'Harpenden Hoppa' for instance could be a new model for this.

It runs 3 days a week, 4 times a day from Roundwood estate to the town centre and back. It is driven by volunteers, and operates as part of the 'Harpenden Connect 'charity.

The vehicle was donated by Herts County Council and refurbished with a new livery. Residents support and use it, and suggested the route which serves all the town's health centres. It is mainly for OAPs but is open to anyone with a £2 flat fare.

Harpenden Hoppa- a new type of community bus model

5. The Present day

The present day has seen a continuing rise in car and road traffic levels, to the point where road pricing and regulation may be needed, as in Singapore where it is very expensive to own and use a private car in the city.

One side effect of the growth in road and air traffic, is a demand for growth in the rail network.

With airport landing slots now at a premium in Europe and airport runway growth a hot political topic and fast reaching saturation point and capacity; and roads also saturated, attention is turning to new rail growth.

In the UK the High Speed 2 rail line and HS3 have created political debate, but are due to start construction soon. This will have the advantage of speeding up longer distance journeys across the UK.

Also Eurostar and DB are planning new routes, such as Amsterdam to compete with short haul airlines, and Frankfurt within 4 hours of London. These are key financial centres and short haul international flying is a slow business.

Schiphol airport is also one of the busiest in Europe for interchange, so freeing up slots would allow growth to new destinations.

Eurostar are also looking at the leisure market, with places such as Geneva and norther Italy being considered which could be an attractive market.

Carmaggedon - what happened in Los Angeles where public transport had to be reintroduced to help reduce grid lock

With public transport we may have to see a change in the way bus services operate in future. This may include a limited daytime commercial bus network, with some evening and Sunday services.

However loss making local services may have to be redesigned as smaller Microbus services, and funded and structured differently to provide either free services for residents or low cost services geared for tourism.

The existing set up where contract services are geared to age old travel patterns and OAPs demands will have to change as they simply won't be around in future?

School and educational services could be funded via the educational budgets, to free up resources for other new services.

We currently have rail replacement services when rail routes are closed for maintenance.

However in future we could see some busy bus routes and crowded roads become rail or tram routes, as in Wimbledon and Croydon where old rail lines were given a new lease of life. Other European cities have followed suit.

Supported public bus services-becoming a thing of the past?

Converting lightly used rail and bus routes to trams has worked well generally where this has been tried.

But a word of warning. The Bus Rapid Transit idea has been a commercial disaster in the UK. Both Luton and St. Ives busways have suffered financial problems and lower demand than anticipated as buses will never be as popular as trams or rail services. That is because they are not regarded as a permanent fixture by the public.

The bus rapid transit idea, also suffers from having guided buses which are more expensive than normal buses, and not as frequent as trams and without the same capacity.

Tram seen at Mitcham stop

The other advantage of trams is that stops can be more frequent than train and are cheaper to construct with low platforms, suited to the elderly or disabled.

They are fuel efficient and an off road system which can run on road in town centres and pedestrian areas, unlike trains. The only disadvantage is having to cross the tracks in practice.

Private school and other bus networks will continue to grow, but road capacity is unlikely to be increased in future due to high construction costs.

Instead we will have to make better use of road space, or end up with 6 land highways in Los Angeles full of traffic going at a crawl all day.

To do this some form of road pricing may be needed, or people encouraged not to use roads and parking areas at peak times. Road pricing is one way of doing this democratically.

Another way is to simply ban non-electric vehicles at certain times from heavily polluted areas.

Whilst buses take up a fair amount of road space, HGVs take up a huge amount of road space. Transferring this to rail systems would remove a lot of congestion which can be accommodated on the rail network. This would free up space for other traffic.

It may be necessary to upgrade rail to handle more freight long term, but this can be done fairly easily with reduced land take compared to a new road scheme or expanded road. Even widening a motorway costs millions per mile.

The Barking-Zhengzhou weekly rail freight service takes a week to arrive but is cost effective. Flying the freight would be costly but arrive within 24 hours. This is usually done for fresh produce only.

Sending freight by sea is cheap, but also polluting as ships still use diesel. However Barking to Zhengzhou by ship would take 6 weeks by comparison. In the current world market place, that may be simply too long.

The majority of car journeys are less than 2 miles. Many of these could be replaced by walking, cycling or other means of transport.

Each mode of transport has its optimum range where it is most (cost) effective.

For instance;

Walking is 0-2 miles

Car is 2-100 miles

Cycling is 2-10 miles

Bus is 3-10 miles

Train is 10-600 miles and

Air is 100-5000 miles

So for instance using a car to do just 1 mile is wasteful, but people still do this. By the time the car has warmed up the journey is over.

Likewise using a plane to fly just 100 miles is wasteful and time consuming, particularly if taking luggage which has to be checked in for security.

Perhaps a campaign of education is needed to show people which is the most cost effective way to travel for a given location.

Conversely cycling 100 miles would be strenuous and take excessive time.

An interesting use of road space occurs at peak times in San Francisco where there is a moveable central barrier or 'Zipper'. This is moved so that the peak flow has an extra lane, whilst the contra flow has one less lane where less busy.

Temporary moveable barriers may be a solution to overcrowded roads in places.

There are ways to combat road congestion such as bus lanes, priority lanes, charging at peak times and switching traffic to other routes if possible.

These all have some effect but the long term solution may be smarter working where you don't travel much at all? You let your smartphone do the work instead.

Parcel deliveries have increased as people want items delivered that they used to shop for. The need to live a 24/7 lifestyle is to blame for excess travel demand.

Perhaps people need to look at their 24/7 lifestyles and see where unnecessary journeys can be simply omitted or combined to avoid duplication, saving the need to travel and risk being stuck in traffic?

I myself have done this and reduced my annual mileage from 25,000 7 years ago to under 10,000 miles a year by car now, so it can be done.

Also people buy multiple cars in some households. Why? If you look at car usage throughout the week, you may be surprised that cars may only be in use occasionally at peak times, and redundant the rest of the time.

Enlightened families share car use so that the family can use the car evenings and weekends to maximise benefit at less busy times, with the breadwinner using rail or other means of transport to commute.

This makes economic sense as simply owning or using a car or vehicle can be an expensive business now.

Vehicle deign may need updating, such as VWs new Microbus which is a modern version of the iconic camper van. 4 x 4s are popular but a combined multi use vehicle may the thing of the future?

The stealth bomber electric mountain bike-the next big thing in transport?

6. Future travel trends

The future is a big place with huge potential. It also carries many risks.

Let's look firstly at what we do know will happen or will not happen:

Large scale airport growth just isn't going to happen as it is politically unpopular. We may get a new runway here or there, but overall airports will be running at or near capacity.

Pricing may resolve this issue with low cost carriers moving to cheaper regional airports with capacity.

That may mean your holiday flight will leave from Stansted rather than Heathrow in future.

It may mean that less busy flights may be merged to save landing slots, and larger planes used to cut down on handling charges.

Plane design is set to change with electric aircraft being mooted and tested. A solar powered plane has already flown around the world, but admittedly was a one person plane.

Airlines are already discouraging people from travelling with large cases in the hold, so that can be freed up for other cargoes. This also saves on fuel.

With a shift towards promoting business travel post Brexit, leisure travel may take a back seat and have to adapt to a changing marketplace.

We have seen that in the past, with low costs carriers coming and going, and destinations being popular, then seeing a slump in demand after adverse news.

We may see a 2 speed market as happened with the postal system. Urgent travel may be at premium rates and expressed, whilst a more sedate mode of travel may be cheaper but slower.

This has led to a rise in popularity of canal boats in recent years by older people, used for both living in at low cost, whilst touring at a more sedate pace.

With housing costs at a premium, alternative modes of both travel and housing are being explored. Containerised housing is being considered for wider use as prefabricated housing, which can be removable if the site is temporary.

Containers of course are used for shipping freight, but can also provide good low cost fast erection modern housing for temporary use or in areas of very high demand such as London.

Shipping containers used to provide attractive low cost fast erection prefabricated housing in future. Reducing the need to travel using Wi-Fi.

With a squeeze on road space, more inventive use of road space will be needed. This can involve road charging, pollution charging, and smaller vehicles to take up less space, moveable barriers to make better use of space in peak hours.

Large scale road building is unlikely unless to remove bottlenecks. So some way of removing unnecessary traffic will be needed. Part of that will be an education campaign such as 'do you really need to drive' or 'is your journey really necessary'?

A recycling scheme for old vehicles is essential, as this would free up road space taken by vehicles that are abandoned or restricting road width unnecessarily.

It is estimated that 10% of vehicles could be recycled, and it could also boost the steel recycling industry and investment in electric arc furnaces.

With buses, smaller is better as they are more sustainable. The use of large buses is only cost-effective on the busiest routes.

Smaller electric or hybrid Microbuses should be introduced to boost low cost services that are lightly used, and reduce fuel costs.

Rail is expanding worldwide, and the construction of new rail routes is continuing, reversing the trend of 50 years ago.

These are high speed purpose built routes for international and high speed domestic traffic. These can also accommodate increased freight use, removing excess heavy goods vehicles from many busy roads.

It is estimated that HGVs can take up and occupy one entire lane of many major road routes. Long distance freight should be incentivised to go by rail, as distribution tends to be by van or even cars locally.

With longer distance fast rail travel in future, the need for short haul airlines should reduce freeing up airport slots for new services which do not compete with medium distance rail up to 600 miles.

There may be a need to develop new style rail services. In the UK for instance we have rail franchises, but we don't have 'national' or international rail services except perhaps for Eurostar, Arriva Trains Wales and Scot rail.

There is a cross country service but this tends to be Scotland to the South West.

There is no Birmingham-Stratford-Ashford service for instance that connects with Eurostar and other international services and the city of London direct which Virgin have expressed interest in.

Harefield Viaduct on High Speed 2. Due to start main construction in 2018.

With smartcards and digital technology, a USB power point and Wi-Fi may be just as important as getting on the train.

Smartphones are the norm now, and it is possible to do business on the train or plane, although phoning whilst on a plane is not easy or universally possible.

When new high speed services are operational, that will free up space on the conventional rail network for faster local services and freight.

That in turn will make it more attractive to develop new services without chewing up valuable road space.

Air services will develop, but may reflect changing demand as high speed rail kicks in by 2025. There may be more mid-range flights from the UK and elsewhere, but a reduction in short haul flights competing with rail.

The airline industry may need to go upmarket to compete with high speed rail, offering comfort and something better than just a basic 'air-bus' service.

On the road car use has been growing relentlessly, with growth in freight too.

There needs to be a recycling scheme to remove old wrecks, dirty smoky vehicles and abandoned cars which take up parking slots, and free up road space generally.

The switch from road to rail freight should also free up road space at busy times. There may need to be an embargo on HGVs and vans using busy roads at peak times.

People will need to look at their car use, so we may need personal travel plans, similar to school travel plans when large numbers of people travel at the same time.

That is a system where we take a typical week and plan all of journeys by car. This would remove the spur of the moment car use, and unnecessary journeys which are so damaging to the environment.

Car clubs go some way towards this idea, but it needs to be centrally co-ordinated to work. If people are penalised for taking unnecessary journeys, then perhaps that will have an effect.

At sea, there is a new generation of warships under construction which are fuel efficient and up to date. These will replace ageing vessels due for the scrapyard.

Older commercial shipping needs updating though as many older ships are still polluting and oil or diesel powered.

The cruise liner market though is very different and has modernised considerably over the last 10 years with some huge, up to the minute vessels with the very latest facilities and technology.

Modern cruise liners are a far cry from the oil smoking ships of the past

For many of us the car will remain the stable mode of transport. The car of the future could look very different though. Multi use multi modal vehicles may be the norm, the old idea of a city car and a country car could well happen.

Transformers has stimulated thinking about vehicles that can mutate into various forms for different purposes. A vehicle that can be modular for instance with parts added or removed is not out of the question.

A car or vehicle that can be adapted for passengers and or freight would be very useful, such as an extended shooting brake. Cars tend to be most used in colder northern climates, with bikes and scooters widely used in warmer, drier climates.

Overall, a balanced transport system is what is needed, but they may need some co-ordination to avoid chaos at peak times of everyone using the system at once causing overload.

If the roads, railways, shipping and airports were evenly used, that can cause problems.

To alleviate that, rail and public transport operators try to price accordingly to dissuade peak travel, and that should continue.

The answer may be some sort of central computer system that regulates traffic usage, either by pricing or allowance so that traffic never reaches saturation level on each mode.

This is where smartcards could come into their own, producing your own travel plan for each journey by computer and print out or ticket and guide as appropriate.

Ideally we would need a combination of a satellite navigation system and a smartcard that could do that, and put it on your smartphone for ease of display.

When that day comes, travel should become a pleasure not a chore?

My phone is my ticket - one day perhaps it may organise all your travel needs?

About the Author;

Paul was 59 at the time of writing this book, and married over 30 years with 3 children, and a grand-daughter; plus an Old English sheepdog puppy called Bella. Paul is a Chartered Surveyor and Engineer by training, with over 40 years' experience.

He is also a voluntary station adopter with the Abbey Line Community rail partnership since its inception in 2005; and has run a voluntary local transport user group since 1986.

He is also a leading UK flight and traditional archer.

Paul has written a number of published and self-published books plus some published articles; including 'My Wonderful Fran', 'Artificial Nocturne', '30 years of bus deregulation' and 'Planning and Development; changing the way we travel.'

All available now on Amazon.

*If you enjoyed reading this story, then perhaps you may enjoy reading other books by the same author;

'My Wonderful Fran', a novel about my late daughter's fight against ASF;

'Artificial Nocturne' a fictional dance story mixing ballet and indie music; and

'30 Years of Bus Deregulation' tracking the story of how bus deregulation has affected travel in the UK with specific reference to the South East;

All are now available on Amazon Kindle.

Thank you for reading this story.

amazon

Printed in Great Britain
by Amazon